D1710212

COUNTRY  PROFILES

# COLOMBIA

BY GOLRIZ GOLKAR

BELLWETHER MEDIA • MINNEAPOLIS, MN

**Blastoff! Discovery** launches a new mission: reading to learn. Filled with facts and features, each book offers you an exciting new world to explore!

BLASTOFF! UNIVERSE

BLASTOFF! Beginners — GRADE K

BLASTOFF! READERS — GRADES 1-3

BLASTOFF! DISCOVERY — GRADE 4

This edition first published in 2021 by Bellwether Media, Inc.

No part of this publication may be reproduced in whole or in part without written permission of the publisher.
For information regarding permission, write to Bellwether Media, Inc.,
Attention: Permissions Department,
6012 Blue Circle Drive, Minnetonka, MN 55343.

Library of Congress Cataloging-in-Publication Data

Names: Golkar, Golriz, author.
Title: Colombia / by Golriz Golkar.
Description: Minneapolis, MN : Bellwether Media, 2021. |
    Series: Country profiles | Includes bibliographical references
    and index.
Audience: Ages 7-13 | Audience: Grades 4-6 | Summary: "Engaging
    images accompany information about Colombia. The combination
    of high-interest subject matter and narrative text is intended for
    students in grades 3 through 8"–Provided by publisher.
Identifiers: LCCN 2020001611 (print) | LCCN 2020001612 (ebook)
    | ISBN 9781644872512 (library binding) | ISBN
    9781681037141 (ebook)
Subjects: LCSH: Colombia–Juvenile literature.
Classification: LCC F2258.5 .G65 2021  (print) | LCC F2258.5
    (ebook) | DDC 986.1–dc23
LC record available at https://lccn.loc.gov/2020001611
LC ebook record available at https://lccn.loc.gov/2020001612

Editor: Rebecca Sabelko    Designer: Brittany McIntosh

Printed in the United States of America, North Mankato, MN.

# TABLE OF CONTENTS

MOUNT MONSERRATE
BOGOTÁ

A family strolls through the morning fog outside the majestic church on Mount Monserrate. They peek inside the chapel to view its famous Christ statue. As they leave, the fog begins to clear. The skyscrapers and orange rooftops of downtown Bogotá slowly appear.

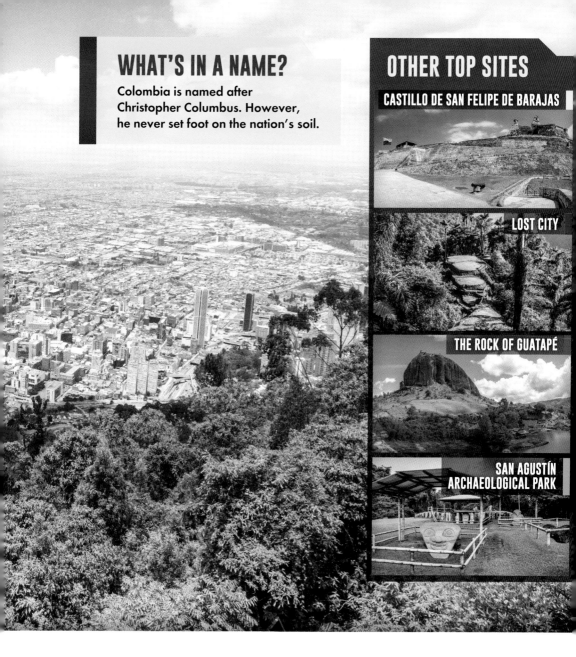

The family takes the **funicular** train downtown. They make their way to the Gold Museum. Along the way, they stop at a café for rich Colombian coffee and thin wafer snacks called *obleas*. Nature, art, and delicious **cuisine** offer a glimpse of Colombia's magic!

5

CARIBBEAN
SEA

BARRANQUILLA

PANAMA

VENEZUELA

MEDELLÍN

PACIFIC
OCEAN

BOGOTÁ

CALI

COLOMBIA

ECUADOR

PERU

SAN ANDRÉS
ISLAND

PROVIDENCIA
ISLAND

BRAZIL

Colombia is located in northwestern South America. It covers 439,736 square miles (1,138,910 square kilometers). The country has borders with the Pacific Ocean to the west and the Caribbean Sea to the north. Panama lies to the northwest and divides the two bodies of water. Venezuela and Brazil are neighbors to the east. Peru and Ecuador share the southern border.

Bogotá, the capital, sits in the nation's center upon a high **plateau** in the northern Andes Mountains. The tiny islands of San Andrés and Providencia are located northwest of the **mainland** in the Caribbean Sea.

# LANDSCAPE AND CLIMATE

Colombia has a **diverse** landscape. Waves splash upon the sandy beaches of the coasts. The **humid** Chocó jungle extends across the Panama border. The Andes Mountains span the west. They extend into three ranges. The Magdalena and Cauca river valleys separate them. Eastern Colombia flattens into the **plains** of Los Llanos. The Amazon **rain forest** makes up the southeast.

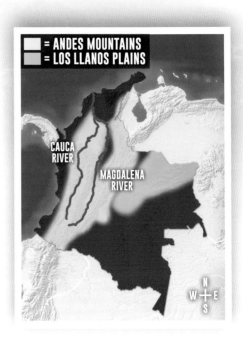

= ANDES MOUNTAINS
= LOS LLANOS PLAINS

CAUCA RIVER

MAGDALENA RIVER

N
W — E
S

LOS LLANOS

ANDES
MOUNTAINS

## BOGOTÁ
Average
seasonal highs
and lows

**JANUARY**
HIGH: 66 °F (19 °C)
LOW: 45 °F (7 °C)

**APRIL**
HIGH: 65 °F (18 °C)
LOW: 49 °F (9 °C)

**JULY**
HIGH: 63 °F (17 °C)
LOW: 48 °F (9 °C)

**OCTOBER**
HIGH: 65 °F (18 °C)
LOW: 47 °F (8 °C)

°F = degrees Fahrenheit
°C = degrees Celsius

## WELCOME TO AMERICA!
Colombia is nicknamed the "gateway to
South America." It sits in the northwestern
part of the continent where South America
connects with Central America.

Colombia has a **tropical** climate. Temperatures
do not vary much throughout the year. Mountainous
regions are cooler than coastal areas. Some areas,
such as the Amazon, receive more than 100 inches
(254 centimeters) of rain per year!

Colombia's varied landscape is home to many kinds of animals. High in the branches of the rain forest, sloths and monkeys find food and shelter. Jaguars roam the land where the rain forest and the plains meet. They search for capybaras or anteaters. Toucans, terns, and **migrating** birds from North America fly over the country.

Rare spectacled bears roam mountain plateaus. The national animal, the Andean condor, soars in the sky above. The Pacific waters are home to humpback whales and sharks. Dolphins, stingrays, and jellyfish swim in the warmer waters of the Caribbean.

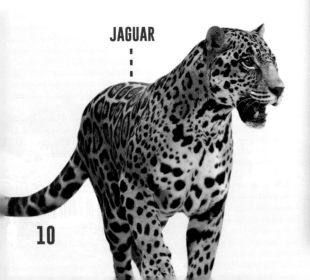

JAGUAR

LINNE'S TWO-TOED SLOTH

BOTTLENOSE DOLPHIN

ANDEAN CONDOR

## BIRD PARADISE

Nearly 2,000 species of birds are found in Colombia.

SPECTACLED BEAR

# SPECTACLED BEAR

Life Span: up to 20 years
Red List Status: vulnerable

spectacled bear range =

| LEAST CONCERN | NEAR THREATENED | VULNERABLE | ENDANGERED | CRITICALLY ENDANGERED | EXTINCT IN THE WILD | EXTINCT |
|---|---|---|---|---|---|---|

More than 49 million people live in Colombia. Around 9 out of every 10 Colombians are white or have mixed European and **native** backgrounds. Some Colombians have African **ancestry** or mixed African and European roots.

Most Colombians are Roman Catholic. A small **minority** is Protestant. Spanish is the official language of Colombia. The nation is home to the third-largest Spanish-speaking population in the world. More than 180 native languages and **dialects** are also spoken around the country.

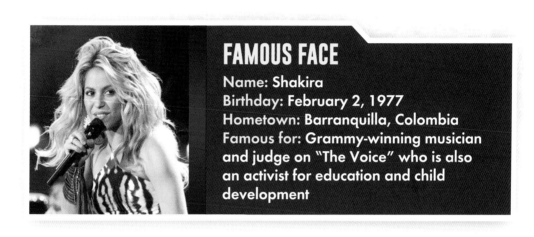

## FAMOUS FACE

Name: Shakira
Birthday: February 2, 1977
Hometown: Barranquilla, Colombia
Famous for: Grammy-winning musician and judge on "The Voice" who is also an activist for education and child development

## SPEAK SPANISH

BOGOTÁ

| ENGLISH | SPANISH | HOW TO SAY IT |
| --- | --- | --- |
| hello | hola | OH-lah |
| goodbye | adiós | ah-dee-OHS |
| please | por favor | pohr fah-VOR |
| thank you | gracias | grah-SEE-ahs |
| yes | sí | SEE |
| no | no | noh |

# COMMUNITIES

Most Colombians live in big cities such as Bogotá, Medellín, and Cali. Buses, subways, and taxis provide transportation. Some residents live in modern apartment buildings. Others live in **slums**. These neighborhoods are crowded and have poorly built homes. Colombians also live in small towns. These *pueblos* are busy but quieter than cities.

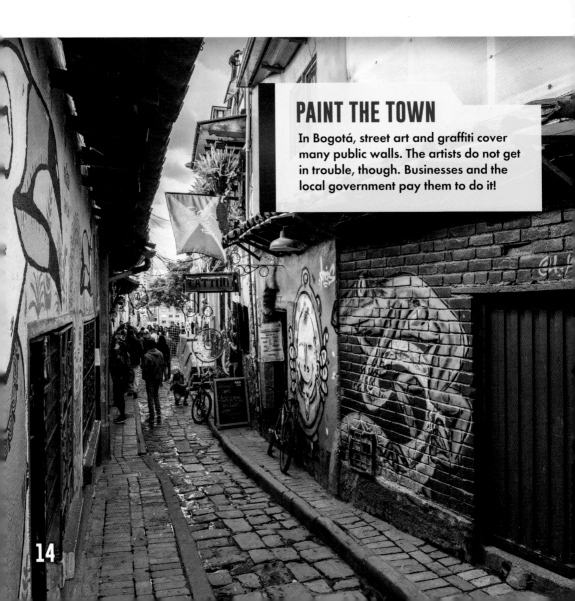

## PAINT THE TOWN

In Bogotá, street art and graffiti cover many public walls. The artists do not get in trouble, though. Businesses and the local government pay them to do it!

CHIVA

**Rural** residents live in small white houses with colorful porches. They are typically made of clay and wood. Colorful buses called *chivas* help people get around. Colombians often have big families. Elderly people may live with their children and grandchildren. Homes are typically small, so families spend a lot of time together.

Colombians typically have two last names. The first one is the father's family name. The second is the mother's family name. But Colombians address each other by the father's family name. They greet one another with a handshake, a hug, or a kiss on the cheek.

Colombians enjoy music and dance. *Cumbia* mixes Spanish, African, and native sounds. Five musicians play **traditional** instruments as colorfully dressed men and women dance to a stepping rhythm. *Vallenato* is another popular musical style that includes vocals.

CUMBIA
DANCERS

## DO YOU SPEAK ENGLISH?

In 2004, the Colombian government made English the main foreign language taught in schools. People believe this will help Colombians get better jobs around the world.

Colombian children must attend school from ages 5 to 15. Public education is free. Students study many subjects including religion, foreign languages, and technology. After high school, some Colombians attend universities or technical schools.

Colombian **social classes** influence the work people do. Most of the population belongs to the lower and middle classes. Many of these Colombians work on coffee, cotton, and sugarcane **plantations**. Some people work in gold mines or steel mills. Many Colombians are small business owners. Upper class citizens may run large businesses, hold government jobs, or work in skilled professions such as law.

GOLD MINER

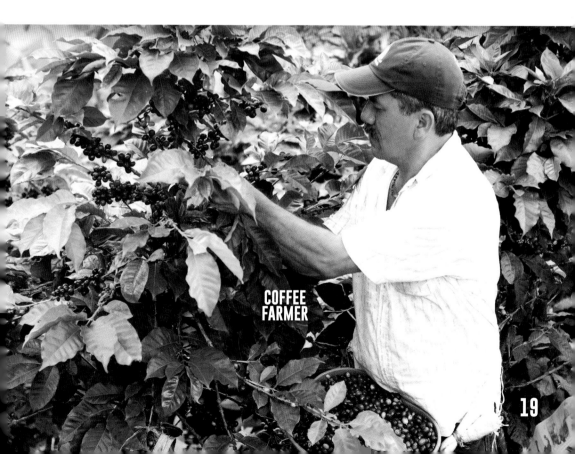

COFFEE FARMER

TOUR OF COLOMBIA

Soccer is the most popular sport in Colombia. The Colombian national team has played in several World Cup tournaments. Baseball and basketball are other popular sports. Colombians also enjoy cycling and watching cycling races. Every year, they cheer on professional cyclists who compete in the 12-day Tour of Colombia race.

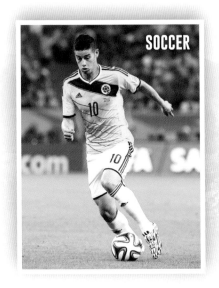

SOCCER

Colombia's beautiful landscape is perfect for outdoor activities. Outside of the busy cities, Colombians enjoy strolling along beaches, hiking, and horseback riding. They also like to play traditional games like *tejo*, the national throwing sport.

TEJO

## TINGO, TANGO

**What You Need:**
- a small object to pass around (like a ball or beanbag)
- a chart of 6 to 8 fun "penalties," such as quack like a duck
- 6 players, including the chanter

**Instructions:**
1. Choose a chanter.
2. The chanter closes their eyes and chants the word "tingo" over and over while everyone else passes the object around.
3. The chanter says "tango" at some point.
4. The player who is holding the object when "tango" is spoken must go to the center of the circle. This player gets a penalty.
5. The player chooses one penalty from the penalty chart. They must act it out.
6. The player returns to the circle and becomes the new chanter.
7. The game begins again.

**COFFEE BREAK**
There are over 500,000 coffee growers in Colombia. The country is the second-largest coffee producer in the world, after Brazil.

*AREPAS*

Colombia's diversity is reflected in its cuisine. *Arepas*, or corn cakes, are a favorite Colombian breakfast. Each region prepares them differently. But they often include cheese. The classic *corrientazo*, or lunch, is the main meal of the day. It includes soup, meat or fish with rice, a salad, and dessert. Dinners are usually light. They include bread and cheese with Colombian coffee.

Rice, meat, potatoes, and beans are Colombian **staples**. Coastal regions enjoy *arroz con coco*, a rice and coconut dish. *Ajiaco*, a chicken and potato soup, is popular in Bogotá. Pork rinds and beans are eaten in Medellín.

ARROZ CON COCO

AJIACO

## POLVOROSAS

Have an adult help you make this sweet treat!

### Ingredients:
1 1/2 cups unsalted butter
1/2 teaspoon vanilla extract
1/2 cup sugar
2 cups all-purpose flour
1/2 cup powdered sugar

### Steps:
1. Preheat the oven to 350 degrees Fahrenheit (177 degrees Celsius).
2. Melt the butter in a medium pot over low heat.
3. Let the butter simmer until foam appears. Remove from heat. Scrape off the foam.
4. Pour the butter into a bowl and mix for 3 minutes with an electric mixer.
5. Add vanilla and sugar and mix until blended. Add flour and mix for 2 minutes more.
6. Form dough into a ball, cover in plastic wrap, and cool for 30 minutes in the refrigerator.
7. Break off 2 tablespoons of dough at a time and roll into small balls. Flatten each ball into a cookie shape on a greased baking sheet.
8. Bake cookies for 20 minutes or until golden. After cooling for 5 minutes, sprinkle powdered sugar over the cookies.

# CELEBRATIONS

Colombians enjoy many holidays throughout the year. In January, the Blacks and Whites' Carnival is held in the city of Pasto. For six days, Colombians celebrate their country's diversity with street parties.
In February, Colombians celebrate the Barranquilla Carnival. Music, dance, and lively parades light up the streets of the city of Barranquilla.

Christmas is a favorite Colombian holiday. It is celebrated for a whole month. Cities are decked out with lights. Fireworks light up the sky. People visit family, attend church, and enjoy traditional foods. Colombians are proud of their rich **heritage**!

BARRANQUILLA CARNIVAL

BLACKS AND WHITES'
CARNIVAL

# TIMELINE

**1499**
Spanish explorer Alonso de Ojeda is the first known European to arrive in Colombia

**1899**
A three-year civil war begins between political groups

**1948**
A second major civil war erupts between political groups

**1819**
The Republic of Gran Colombia is founded after Colombians defeat the Spanish army and win independence

**1903**
Panama separates from Colombia

**1830**
Venezuela and Ecuador split from Gran Colombia, leading present-day Colombia and Panama to become New Granada

**1970s**
Dangerous illegal activities begin to increase within Colombia and last for several decades

**2017**
Pope Francis encourages Colombians to seek peace during his visit to the country

**2010**
Colombia receives 1.4 million foreign visitors as safety improves in the country

**1982**
Colombian author Gabriel García Márquez wins the Nobel Prize in Literature

**Official Name:** Republic of Colombia

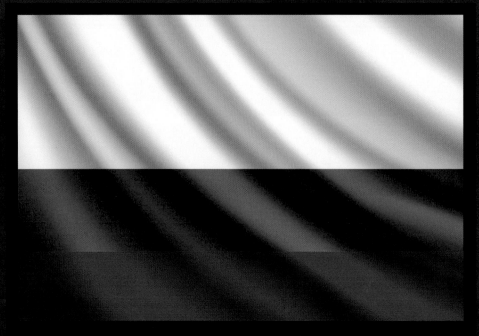

**Flag of Colombia:** The Colombian flag has three horizontal bands. The top double-width band of yellow represents the country's gold, the middle blue band represents its seashores, and the bottom red band represents the blood spilled during the wars fought for freedom.

**Area:** 439,736 square miles
(1,138,910 square kilometers)

**Capital City:** Bogotá

**Important Cities:** Medellín, Cali, Barranquilla

**Population:**
49,084,841 (July 2020)

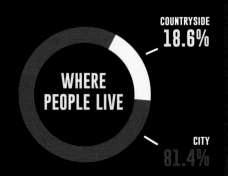

WHERE PEOPLE LIVE

COUNTRYSIDE **18.6%**

CITY **81.4%**

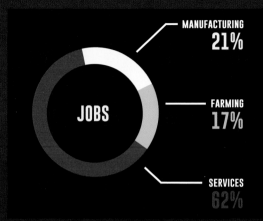

MANUFACTURING
21%

**JOBS**

FARMING
17%

SERVICES
62%

**Main Exports:**

oil

coal

coffee

gold

**National Holiday:**
Independence Day (July 20)

**Main Language:**
Spanish

**Form of Government:**
presidential republic

**Title for Country Leader:**
president

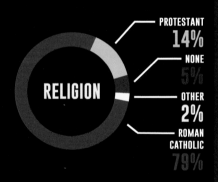

PROTESTANT
14%

NONE
5%

OTHER
2%

ROMAN
CATHOLIC
79%

**RELIGION**

**Unit of Money:**
Colombian peso

# GLOSSARY

**ancestry**—a line of relatives who lived long ago

**cuisine**—a style of cooking

**dialects**—local ways of speaking particular languages

**diverse**—made up of people or things that are different from one another

**funicular**—related to a railway that uses a cable and balanced cars to go up and down a mountainside

**heritage**—the traditions, achievements, and beliefs that are part of the history of a group of people

**humid**—damp or moist

**mainland**—a continent or main part of a continent

**migrating**—traveling from one place to another, often with the seasons

**minority**—related to a group of people who are different from a larger group in a country

**native**—originally from the area or related to a group of people that began in the area

**plains**—large areas of flat land

**plantations**—large farms that grow coffee beans, cotton, rubber, or other crops; plantations are mainly found in warm climates.

**plateau**—an area of flat, raised land

**rain forest**—a thick, green forest that receives a lot of rain

**rural**—related to the countryside

**slums**—parts of cities that are crowded or have poor housing

**social classes**—broad groups in society having common economic, cultural, or political status

**staples**—widely used foods or other items

**traditional**—related to customs, ideas, or beliefs handed down from one generation to the next

**tropical**—part of the tropics; the tropics is a hot, rainy region near the equator.

# TO LEARN MORE

## AT THE LIBRARY

Barghoorn, Linda. *Returning to Colombia*. New York, N.Y.: Crabtree Publishing Company, 2020.

Klepeis, Alicia Z. *Peru*. Minneapolis, Minn.: Bellwether Media, 2019.

Regan, Michael. *South America*. Lake Elmo, Minn.: Focus Readers, 2020.

## ON THE WEB

# FACTSURFER

Factsurfer.com gives you a safe, fun way to find more information.

1. Go to www.factsurfer.com.

2. Enter "Colombia" into the search box and click $\mathbb{Q}$.

3. Select your book cover to see a list of related content.

31

# INDEX

The images in this book are reproduced through the courtesy of: Daniel Conde/ Getty Images, front cover; Zoonar GmbH/ Alamy Stock Photo, pp. 4-5; Fotos593, pp. 5 (Castillo de San Felipe de Barajas), 13 (bottom); Scott Biales DitchtheMap, p. 5 (Lost City); Karol Kozolwski, p. 5 (San Agustín Archaeological Park); iFerol, p. 5 (The Rock of Guatapé); Luc Kohnen, p. 8; ostill is Franck Camhi, p. 9 (top); rafcha, p. 9 (bottom); Anan Kaewkhammul, p. 10 (jaguar); Vladimir Wrangel, p. 10 (sloth); Tory Kallman, p. 10 (dolphin); Don Mammoser, p. 10 (condor); Christian Musat, p. 11; dbimages/ Alamy Stock Photo, p. 12; Sean Nel, p. 13 (top); Karol Kozolowski Premium RM Collection/ Alamy Stock Photo, p. 14; Jeffery Isaac Greenberg 10/ Alamy Stock Photo, p. 15; Michael Spring/ Alamy Stock Photo, p. 16; jfbenning, p. 17; Roberto Orrú/ Alamy Stock Photo, p. 18; Perla Sofia, p. 19 (top); mauritius Images GmbH/ Alamy Stock Photo, p. 19 (bottom); Karloz Monsalve, p. 20 (top); A. Ricardo, p. 20 (bottom); Nowaczyk, p. 21 (top); Sergy Novikov, p. 21 (bottom); amenic181, p. 22 (coffee); agefotostock/ Alamy Stock Photo, p. 22; rukowskii/ Alamy Stock Photo, p. 23 (top); AS Food studio, p. 23 (middle); Panther Media GmbH/ Alamy Stock Photo, p. 23 (bottom); Kobby Dagan, p. 24; Orchin photo, p. 25; North Wind Picture Archives/ Alamy Stock Photo, p. 26; Wenn US/ Alamy Stock Photo, p. 27 (top); Ulf Andersen/ Contributor/ Getty Images, p. 27 (bottom); PvE/ Alamy Stock Photo, p. 29 (banknote); Fat Jackey, p. 29 (coin).